A guide to collecting and analysing information for Form C (England)

Paul Adams

coramBAAF
ADOPTION & FOSTERING ACADEMY

Published by
CoramBAAF Adoption and Fostering Academy
41 Brunswick Square
London WC1N 1AZ
www.corambaaf.org.uk

Coram Academy Limited, registered as a company limited by guarantee in England and Wales number 9697712, part of the Coram group, charity number 312278

© CoramBAAF 2017

British Library Cataloguing in Publication Data
A catalogue record for this book is available from the British Library

ISBN 978 1 910039 63 2

Project management by Jo Francis, Publications, CoramBAAF
Designed and typeset by Helen Joubert Design
Printed in Great Britain by the Lavenham Press

All rights reserved. Apart from any fair dealing for the purposes of research or private study, or criticism or review, as permitted under the Copyright, Designs and Patents Act 1988, this publication may not be reproduced, stored in a retrieval system, or transmitted in any form or by any means, without the prior written permission of the publishers.

The moral right of the author has been asserted in accordance with the Copyright, Designs and Patents Act 1988.

For the latest news on CoramBAAF titles and special offers, sign up to our free publications bulletin at https://corambaaf.org.uk/subscribe.

Contents

1 How to use this guide — 1
Introduction — 1
Structure of Form C — 1
Content and purpose of this guide — 3

2 The context of assessment — 5
Research evidence — 5
Safeguarding — 5
The issues for family and friends carers — 6
The context of assessment — 7
Collaborative working — 7

3 Descriptive information — 9
Description and personality — 9
Identity — 10
Family history — 11
Education and employment — 13
Previous relationships — 15

4 Relationships and network — 17
The couple relationship — 17
The household — 19
Wider family/significant others — 22
Support network — 23

5 Parenting capacity — 25
Experience of caring for children — 25
Applicant's relationship with the child — 26
Ability to meet the needs of the child — 27
Contact and family relationships — 29

6 Checks and references — 31
DBS check — 31
Local authority check/previous applications to foster or adopt — 32
Health — 33
Home and neighbourhood — 35
Income and expenditure — 36
Previous family court proceedings — 37
Personal references — 37
Other checks and references — 39

7 The different legal orders 41
Understanding the legal framework 41
Special guardianship 42
Fostering 42

Bibliography 44

Appendix: family tree and ecomap 46
Drawing a family tree 46
Example of a family tree 47
Drawing an ecomap 48
Example of an ecomap 49

Acknowledgements

My main acknowledgement must be to Roger Chapman whose *Undertaking Fostering Assessments* established the successful format for this series of guides. In writing this guide, I have at times taken and adapted material from that original text. I am also grateful to Roger Chapman and Liz Cooke for reading and commenting on earlier drafts of the guide, and to Jo Francis and Shaila Shah for their publications expertise.

Note about the author

Paul Adams qualified as a social worker in 1993, having been inspired by working as a foster carer in the US, and has worked predominantly in local authority children's services, managing child care and fostering teams. He is an experienced Chair of fostering and adoption panels, interim manager, consultant, trainer, and an adopter.

Paul joined BAAF (now CoramBAAF) as a Fostering Development Consultant in 2010. He has authored Good Practice Guides on parent and child fostering, contact in permanent placements, social work with Gypsy, Roma and Traveller children, and dogs and pets in fostering and adoption. Paul has developed Form C (connected persons), Form FR (fostering reviews) with accompanying good practice guidance, and considerably revised Form F (fostering assessments) in England.

Paul lives in North Wales with his partner Sarah, daughters Louisha and Sherissa, and rescue dog Simba.

Introduction

This guide is designed to help social workers conduct a comprehensive assessment of connected persons or prospective family and friends carers as foster carers or special guardians. It is to be used by assessing social workers in England to complete Form C, published by CoramBAAF in 2017.

The guide is primarily based on Section C of Form C, which requires information about the applicant/s – historical and current – and how that is relevant to their suitability to be foster carers or special guardians for known children. The form requires a range of descriptive information about the applicant/s, information about their relationships and networks, and consideration of their parenting capacity. Chapter 7 is designed to help assessors complete Section D of Form C.

Form C is designed to be presented to fostering panels in relation to foster carers, and to courts when considering special guardianship. It is expected that assessing social workers reading this guide will be familiar with Form C, and the accompanying guidance notes, but it is worth providing a brief overview.

Form C is used solely within England and so this guide is valid for the same area.

Structure of Form C

Front sheet

The front sheet provides basic information about the case, including court details (where relevant) and information about the assessing social workers. There is space for a genogram of the family and a brief summary and recommendation.

Section A – The child

Section A provides information about the child or children, including the circumstances of them becoming looked after, their needs including in relation to contact, and their wishes and feelings.

Section B – The birth family

Section B provides information about the birth family and only needs to be completed for special guardianship assessments.

Section C – The applicant/s

Section C considers information about the applicant/s and is set out in sections that address: personal and family details; descriptive information; relationships and network; parenting capacity; and checks and references.

Section D – either:

- Section D – Temporary approval
- Section D – Special guardianship
- Section D – Fostering

Section D consists of three different forms; only one of these should be selected and completed, according to the type of assessment being undertaken.

Section E – Information checklist

Section E is designed to be used as an aid in gathering information and as a checklist for the assessor and their supervisor. Any relevant information that is gathered should have been included in Section C of the report. It is suggested that Section E is included in the paperwork presented to fostering panels, but it is not designed to be presented with special guardianship reports to court.

Additional tools and resources

There are two sets of tools and resources provided to help the assessor with planning, collecting and presenting some of the information required for this report.

Additional tools and resources (Form C):

1. Application form
2. Assessment agreement
3. Applicant report
4. Chronology
5. Second opinion report
6. Panel member notes
7. Decision form

Additional tools and resources (checks and references):

1. Consent to checks and references form
2. Personal reference form
3. Interview record and analysis form
4. Home safety checklist
5. Dog assessment form
6. Pet assessment form
7. Financial statement and checklist
8. Former partner check form
9. Employment and voluntary activity form
10. School and nursery reference form

These additional tools and resources should be used at the discretion of the assessor and in line with local policies and procedures.

Content and purpose of this guide

After setting out some general guidance about assessing connected persons/family and friends carers, this guide takes Section C of the CoramBAAF Form C, considers each sub-section and looks at how these might be explored with the applicant. This includes:

- a list of questions that can be asked of the applicant or can be used to facilitate further discussion in order to collect some of the basic information required for the purposes of the assessment;

- some suggestions for how the information collected can be analysed to see if it may provide evidence that could be positive for fostering or special guardianship, or could be seen as a potential area of concern or vulnerability by the assessing social worker;

- for some of the areas covered, consideration about how the information given could be verified from sources both within and outside of the family.

Sections from the guidance notes that accompany the CoramBAAF Form C have been repeated in this guide, providing general guidance to accompany the suggested list of questions for that area. It is hoped that by making use of this guide, the assessor will be able to collect the information that will form the basis of a sound assessment.

However, having collected the information, the guide places an emphasis on the analysis of the information collected and consideration of how this is relevant in reaching a judgement about suitability as a foster carer or special guardian. It is important to ensure that the analysis is integrated into the assessment and is used to reach a well-informed, evidence-based assessment.

UNDERTAKING A CONNECTED PERSON/FAMILY AND FRIENDS ASSESSMENT

The information in the Appendix is intended to assist the assessor. This consists of advice on how to present a family tree, and an ecomap pictorially setting out the applicant's support networks.

This guide is not intended to be a quick and easy way of undertaking an assessment. It offers a way of collecting the basic information needed to complete the process. Although most of the guide is presented in question format, it is not intended that the questions merely be fired at the applicant. Rather, they are designed to help the assessor cover key areas in what should be a dynamic process rather than one that consists merely of answers to questions or the completion of a checklist. The assessor must be alert to the idiosyncrasies and complexities of each applicant they assess and be prepared to pursue different lines of questioning and exploration accordingly, and to analyse that information in terms of its relevance to fostering or special guardianship.

Nor should the guide lead to any standardisation of assessments. It is important for assessors to maintain their individual styles of seeking, analysing and presenting information. The guide should be seen as a tool to help in the assessment process and not an end in itself.

Research evidence

While it is not the purpose of this guide to look in any detail at the research evidence behind connected persons/family and friends assessments and placements, it is worth highlighting a few salient points that are essential for assessing social workers to understand. Most crucially, the broad findings from research show that where children cannot live with their parents, they do best across a range of measures if they can live with family and friends carers, be they foster carers or special guardians. Research also shows that these carers are often older, poorer and less healthy than unrelated foster carers, but this has no adverse impact on outcomes for the children whom they look after. This is not to say that support is unnecessary; on the contrary, the research suggests a number of areas where better support could contribute to better outcomes for children, including financial support, help with contact, and provision of therapeutic services for both the child and the adults looking after them.

It is also important to know that issues such as quality of accommodation and early life experiences of the carer are not a good predictor of subsequent outcomes for the children, and the only reliable predictor of the success or otherwise of a placement is the assessment of parenting capacity. It is crucial, therefore, that the assessment recognises this as the key aspect, and does not over-emphasise other aspects. It is also important that the assessment should focus on the applicant's ability to parent that particular child – not children generally – and this will need to be seen in the context of that child's known and likely future developmental needs, and the prospective carer's existing relationship with that child.

Safeguarding

A number of recent Serious Case Reviews have highlighted tragic consequences where unsuitable family and friends carers have been granted special guardianship orders.

- In January 2016, a Serious Case Review in Devon (Staunton, 2016) found evidence of toddler Bonnie having been sexually abused by her grandfather while in the care of her special guardian grandmother, who was fully aware of the risk he posed.

- In February 2017, a Serious Case Review considered the death of Keegan Downer in Birmingham (Wate, 2017) at the hands of her special guardian aunt. Keegan, at 18 months old, had over 150 injuries, and the assessment of her aunt was described as 'striking in its superficiality'.

- In March 2017, a Serious Case Review in Oxfordshire (Harrington, 2017) described how Child A and Child B suffered serious physical and sexual abuse at the hands of connected persons who had been assessed as suitable to look after them.

- In April 2017, a Serious Case Review into the case of seven-year-old Shanay Walker in Nottingham (Wiffin, 2017) raised questions about the quality of the assessment of her aunt as a special guardian. Shanay died with more than 50 separate injuries.

While these cases are clearly not representative of the vast majority of connected person or family and friends carers, they serve to highlight why assessments need to be in-depth and robust, and on a par with those undertaken for prospective adopters and foster carers.

The issues for family and friends carers

Good practice in assessing family and friends carers involves recognising that the issues are not the same as they are for strangers being assessed to foster and adopt. There are a number of key points to consider when assessing this group of carers.

Timing, process and motivation

Family and friends usually find themselves in a situation of being considered to foster or otherwise care for a relative or friend, rather than having actively sought to do this at a time of their choosing. This means that they will not have had time to consider the situation in depth, will often not have received much information about local authority assessment processes, and see themselves as stepping in to help a known child, rather than wanting to become part of a professional child care network. For assessors, it is therefore important to ensure that applicants are provided with good quality information and advice, and alerted to the existence of the various groups and organisations that might assist them. It also means taking the time to explain how an assessment takes place, and encouraging full participation in this process.

Relationships with the child's network

Family and friends will also often, by definition, be looking after a child who is a relative or friend, and as such will be a member of this child's network that often includes their birth parents. The majority of family and friends carers are grandparents, and that means that a birth parent will be their son or daughter. While this can be seen as a positive factor in an application, it can also create some challenging dynamics, and assessors need to be mindful of this. A good assessment will need to explore this aspect in detail, being sensitive to the feelings involved, but also ensuring that the safety of the child is paramount. It should not be assumed that potential carers are best placed to manage any existing or proposed contact arrangements – sometimes they are, but sometimes they are not – and this will need to be assessed on a case-by-case basis. It will also be necessary to look at whether a family group conference has been held, and whether this might be of value.

Power dynamics

Family and friends can be seen as disadvantaged and disempowered when compared to potential "stranger" foster carers. They can only be considered by the one local authority that is involved with the child in question, and cannot decide to approach another local authority or independent fostering provider (IFP) if they are not deemed suitable. Furthermore, some social workers may be tempted to see them as potentially unsuitable carers or parents because they come from the same "problematic" network as the child's birth parents, and in the case of grandparents, having raised those birth parents. This creates both significant feelings (Tarrant et al, 2017) and a power dynamic in the relationship between assessor and applicant/s that needs to be acknowledged and worked with throughout the assessment.

Support needs

The law requires that the local authority must give priority to family and friends carers, and in practice this means that the assessment should include a consideration of the support needs of an applicant, in order that they can effectively care for a child. This may relate to the fact that these carers have usually not planned for this new caring role, with the financial and other implications this brings. Additionally, we know that family and friends carers are often older, have poorer health, and have the additional issue of being a part of the child's family network. All of these things might contribute to support needs – financial, practical and emotional.

Factors that may mean that a stranger is not suitable to foster might not mean that someone is unsuitable to look after a relative or friend, as any negative factors will need to be weighed against the benefits of the child remaining within their existing network or family. In this context, the assessment will need to consider what additional support might reasonably be provided to make the placement work.

Collaborative working

Simmonds (2011) suggests that all assessments, including those of family and friends, need to combine four elements:

- they need to be conducted in a spirit of enquiry;
- they need to be conducted in a spirit of partnership;

- they need to remain focused on the child and their needs and development;
- they need to be written with authority, be evidence-based, and include analysis of the evidence.

All of these elements are necessary in completing Form C, and the need to work collaboratively with applicants is worth highlighting. Good practice suggests that the social worker should discuss with the carers how they would feel most comfortable providing the information requested of them; this could include providing written evidence as well as having discussions with the social worker. However it is achieved, it is essential that the applicant's views and feelings are clearly set out within the report.

One of the tools provided with Form C is an Applicant's Report that allows carers and prospective carers to provide information in their own words. It is strongly recommended that assessing social workers encourage the use of these forms, and provide support to family and friends carers in completing them. It can be hugely helpful to fostering panel members and others if they can see the actual words of the applicant/s, as part of the paperwork submitted. However, use of this particular report does not in any way negate the need for the social worker to ensure that the views of the family and friends carer/s are represented, assessed and analysed throughout the assessment.

A good assessment will be one that is completed in a partnership between the assessor and the person or persons being assessed, and will fully involve others, including children and adults living in that household. While Form C is designed in a way that aims to help assessors remain focused on the key areas that are relevant, and tries to emphasise the importance of partnership, no format can ensure a collaborative working relationship – this is for the individual worker to achieve, with a shared commitment from the person being assessed.

Form C has been designed as a social work assessment, and – as with all social work assessments – there is an expectation that it does more than simply record factual information and set out the views of relevant persons. While this is important, social workers are additionally expected to help the applicant/s to reflect on and explore their position, and the report should include assessment and analysis rather than simply stating what others have said. This cannot be emphasised too strongly.

Description and personality

Although required by regulations, this should not be an overly lengthy section in the report. Comments about the applicant's personality and lifestyle should be included based on their self-reporting, views of their partner (if they have one), views of birth children where the applicant/s have children, and from the range of references and other information available. It will be important to check that a consistent picture is emerging from all these sources and to explore matters further if this is not the case.

- How would you describe yourself?
- What do you feel are your strengths and weaknesses?
- How might others, including your partner if you have one, describe you?
- What evidence can you give to show that you are reliable and dependable?
- Describe your household routine during the week and at weekends.
- What leisure activities do family members enjoy, individually and as a family?
- How is affection displayed in your family?
- How does your family deal with feelings? Are these discussed?
- How have you managed stressful episodes in your life?

ASSESSOR'S ANALYSIS

- **What personal qualities does the applicant have that might make them suitable to care for the child?**
- **Are there any potential areas of emotional vulnerability in relation to taking on the care of the child?**
- **How flexible or rigid is this family with regards to routines and how will the child experience this?**

- **Will this family be sensitive to the child and help them deal with their feelings and emotions?**

> **Verify through:**
> - **Interviews with the child (if of an age and understanding)**
> - **Personal references including from family members**
> - **Employer and former employer checks**
> - **Former partner references**
> - **Social media checks**

Identity

In considering identity, the assessor should start with the applicant/s and consider how they define themselves in terms of ethnicity, culture, religion and sexuality, amongst other areas. The implications of this can then be considered in relation to the identity of the child whom they wish to care for, and their ability to meet the identity needs of that child.

Statutory guidance requires that foster carers 'should ensure that full attention is paid to the individual child's gender, faith, ethnic origin, cultural and linguistic background, sexual orientation and any disability they might have'. This is no less important for prospective special guardians.

If the child is disabled, it is hoped that the applicant/s will be able to demonstrate that they have given proper consideration to the importance of advocacy, promoting rights and challenging discrimination, but if not they will need to be supported to develop this knowledge and ultimately implement a social model of disability.

- How would you describe your own identity in terms of gender, language, ethnicity, disability, class, culture, sexuality and religion?
- Are these important to you and if so, how and why?
- Do you follow any particular religion or faith and how is this incorporated into your lifestyle?
- How would you describe the ethnic and cultural mix of your local community?
- Have you ever experienced prejudice or discrimination?
- How would you describe the identity of the child whom you wish to care for in terms of gender, language, ethnicity, disability, class, culture, sexuality and religion?
- Is their identity the same or different to yours, and if different, how?
- How do you think you could promote the child's identity?

Descriptive information

- Do you think the child has experienced or is likely to experience prejudice or discrimination within the extended family network or wider society?
- How would you feel if the child was gay, lesbian, bisexual or trans?

ASSESSOR'S ANALYSIS

- **Does the applicant understand the identity of the child whom they wish to care for, in terms of ethnicity, culture and the like, and their identity needs arising from this?**
- **Will the applicant be able to advocate for the child and appropriately challenge prejudice and discrimination if necessary?**
- **If the child is disabled, will the applicant be able to promote a social model of disability?**
- **Does the applicant demonstrate a willingness to learn about identity issues as appropriate to the child whom they wish to care for?**
- **Do the applicants display inflexible, judgemental or discriminatory thinking, and if so, how might this impact on the care of the child?**
- **What training or support might the applicant need to meet the identity needs of the child whom they wish to care for?**

> **Verify through:**
> - **Interviews with the child (if of an age and understanding)**
> - **Personal references including from family members**
> - **Social media checks**

Family history

Consideration of family history will entail looking at relationships with parents, siblings and other significant family members. Social workers should consider the coherence, economy and specificity of the applicant's account, and the extent to which they continue to be preoccupied with the past, dismiss its significance or are confused or uncertain about its meaning to them. It is important to be sensitive to cultural differences in styles and models of parenting.

The assessing social worker should have completed a family tree (see Appendix) as part of the front sheet paperwork and this will be helpful. It might also be useful to compile a chronology of life events.

- Where were you born and raised?

- Describe your mother and the nature of your relationship with her.
- Describe your father and the nature of your relationship with him.
- Describe any other significant caregivers or adults in your childhood.
- Describe your relationship with your siblings when growing up.
- As a child, to whom did you feel closest, and why?
- What good things do you remember about your childhood?
- What unhappy memories do you have, such as rejection, upset, illness or hurt?
- Was there anyone who helped you during difficult times?
- How would you describe your overall experience of early childhood?
- What are your significant memories of your teenage years?
- How would you describe your overall experience of adolescence?
- What was your overall experience of being parented?
- In which ways are you like your parents and how are you different?
- How do you feel your experiences as a child have shaped the person you are today?

ASSESSOR'S ANALYSIS

In thinking about these issues, the assessor needs to be careful not to over-simplify the issues, and must be mindful that having a happy childhood is not in itself a good indicator of subsequent parenting ability. Prospective family and friends carers will often have had difficult pasts, and the assessing social worker will need to come to a view about the extent to which the applicant/s has resolved past traumas or losses; shown the capacity to make and sustain close relationships; is able to empathise and understand other people's feelings; and is able to reflect on emotive matters. It is important to remember that family history is only important insofar as it links to how the applicant manages relationships in the present, and how this impacts on capacity to meet the needs of the particular child under consideration.

- **Has the applicant been able to provide a coherent and reflective account of their childhood?**
- **What is the applicant's experience of attachment to parents or other caregivers?**
- **Does the applicant have insight into how their childhood experience has impacted on how they are as adults today?**
- **Where an applicant has experienced loss, abuse or neglect, is there evidence to show that they have been able to overcome this?**

- **How will childhood experiences impact on the parenting capacity of the applicant?**

> **Verify through:**
> - **Personal references including from family members**

Education and employment

Education

This section asks about the applicant's education in a general way, and information about their ability to meet the educational needs of the child whom they wish to care for is covered in a later section (Chapter 5). Repeating the same information in an assessment is unhelpful and should be avoided. The assessor should cross-reference where appropriate.

- Which schools did you attend, and what was your experience of them?
- What was the attitude of your parents towards education?
- Did you go on to further or higher education?
- What educational qualifications did you achieve?
- How would you assess your literacy skills and computer skills?
- Do you have a computer and access to the internet?
- What is your attitude to education as a parent or carer?
- Have you supported a child (other than the child whom you wish to care for) with their education, and if so, what did that entail?

ASSESSOR'S ANALYSIS

- **How will their own experience of education impact on their ability and willingness to support a child's education?**
- **Does the applicant have adequate literacy and computer skills to support a child's education, or will they need support with that?**

> **Verify through:**
> - **Personal references including from family members**

Employment

In relation to employment, the regulations require both historical and current information. Although historical information can usually be provided quite succinctly, possibly referring to a chronology, current information will need to focus on the implications of work for the caring role. It is important not to assume that working is incompatible with child care, but to carefully consider the issues in each individual case. It is not in a child's best interest to be living in a poverty-stricken household, and local authorities should consider whether they can provide appropriate support to allow potential carers to continue to work outside the home.

- Provide details of your employment from leaving school to the present day, and explain any gaps.
- What are your current work arrangements and are these compatible with caring for the child?
- Do you have any plans to change working arrangements, and if so, have you discussed these with your employer?
- If you propose to leave work or reduce your hours in order to care for the child, how will that impact on family finances?
- If you are continuing to work, do you have arrangements in place for school holidays or if the child is ill?

ASSESSOR'S ANALYSIS

- Are there any patterns in the applicant's employment history that are concerning, or any unexplained gaps?
- Does the applicant's work evidence any skills and experiences that might be relevant to their suitability to care for the child?
- If the applicant/s proposes to continue working, do they have a workable plan for caring for the child alongside this, including arrangements for school holidays and if the child is ill?
- If the applicant/s plans to leave work or reduce their hours, will they have an income that is sufficient to meet the child's needs?
- What support might be needed to enable continued employment or to provide financial assistance if they are ceasing or reducing paid work?

Verify through:
- **Chronology**
- **Personal references**
- **Employer or former employer checks**

Previous relationships

At the most basic level, information will be evident from documents such as marriage and civil partnership certificates, but additionally it is important to ascertain the applicant's perspective on the nature of the relationship. In deciding how far to go in considering previous relationships, the assessing social worker will be led by the local authority policy, as well as the particular circumstances of the case.

- Have you had any previous relationships?
- Who was the relationship with?
- How long did it last (when did it start and finish)?
- What was the status of the relationship?
- Why did the relationship end?
- Was there any domestic abuse/violence during the relationship?
- What contact do you have now with your former partner?
- Can we contact the former partner for a reference?
- If not, what are the reasons for this?

Where children were the result of the relationship, or living with the applicant during the relationship, there will be additional matters to consider:

- Were there any children from or living with you in this relationship?
- Who did they live with after the relationship ended, and how was this decided?
- How were the children affected by the break-up and how did you help them deal with this?
- Did you have subsequent contact with the children and how was this organised?
- What contact do you have now with these children?
- If the children stay with you, how often does that happen and where do they sleep?
- How will this be affected by your plans to take on the care of another child?
- What do the children from the previous relationship think about you wanting to care for another child now?
- How will you meet the needs of these children alongside the child you now wish to care for?

ASSESSOR'S ANALYSIS

- **Is the applicant's account corroborated by former partner references and/or by personal referees who knew them both?**

- Are there any emerging patterns from previous relationships, or the ending of those relationships, that might be relevant to the applicant's current relationship?

- If the applicant/s has maintained contact with children from a previous relationship, what does this say about their reliability and commitment?

- How have the needs of children from a previous relationship been considered in relation to the current application?

> **Verify through:**
> - **Personal references including from family members**
> - **Former partner references**
> - **Marriage/civil partnership certificates (where appropriate)**

Relationships and network

4

The couple relationship

The assessment of the stability and permanence of a couple's relationship should include the history of that relationship, how well it works, and the couple's commitment to each other. It should explore what has tested the relationship, and how the partners support each other.

It will be necessary to consider how well the relationship works for both parties, to look at vulnerabilities, and to reflect with the applicants about the potential impact of caring for the child on their relationship. As a part of this discussion, the assessor should be thinking with the applicants about how caring for this child might impact on their current lifestyle; what might need to change, and how any changes will need to be managed. It is about trying to make sure that the applicants are as prepared as they can be, are realistic, and have a full understanding of the likely impact on them.

In assessing a couple, it will be necessary to consider their approach to parenting, as it will be important that they have a shared understanding and an ability to work effectively together. If there has been any domestic abuse in the relationship, this will need detailed and careful consideration.

- How, where and when did you meet your current partner, and how did the relationship develop?
- How would you describe each other?
- What role does each of you have in the relationship, and in the household?
- What qualities do each of you bring to the relationship, and do you have similar or complementary qualities?
- How do you show affection to each other?
- How do you support each other?
- What do you see as the strengths of the relationship?
- What do you feel makes the relationship successful?
- How do you make decisions as a couple? Can you give examples of this?

- How easy do you find it to talk about your feelings or concerns?

- How do you deal with problems and disagreements individually and as a couple? Can you give examples of this?

- Have you had any periods of separation?

- Has there ever been any domestic abuse/violence in your relationship?

- What do your respective families think about your relationship?

- What are the vulnerable areas in your relationship?

- Have you thought about how caring for this child might affect your relationship?

ASSESSOR'S ANALYSIS

- **What is the evidence about the stability and security of this relationship?**

- **Is there evidence of mutual support and understanding of each other's needs?**

- **Is there evidence that this relationship is strong enough to deal with the stresses of caring for the child?**

- **Are there areas of vulnerability in the relationship that could be tested by the child joining the family?**

> **Verify through:**
> - **Personal references including from family members**
> - **Marriage/civil partnership certificates (where appropriate)**

Single applicants

It is important to recognise that single applicants can make excellent carers, and not being in a relationship can bring advantages as well as disadvantages. More information is provided in Betts (2007). When considering a single applicant, it is important to ask:

- Do you envisage being in a couple relationship in the future?

- How do you think that might impact on the child living with you?

- How would you manage that?

The household

This section asks the assessor to provide information about all other household members, adults and children, and their relationship with the child under consideration. It is helpful for the assessor to provide a brief pen picture of all household members, describing personality, ethnicity and the current education or employment of each person. Everyone in the household should be interviewed as part of the assessment, and information from these interviews should usually be set out in this section. It is the relationship that these individuals have with each other and with the child that needs to be considered. In providing information about lifestyle, the assessor has the opportunity to provide a good picture of the family in day-to-day life, describing how a child does, or potentially might, experience living in the home.

Children of the household

- What is the relationship between you and each child in the household?
- Describe the personality and character of each child.
- Describe their lifestyle and interests.
- How is each child doing at nursery, school or college?
- Can we seek a reference from these organisations?
- Has any child been involved with children's services or mental health services?
- If so, can we seek a reference from these services?
- How do the children within the household get on with each other?
- What do the children think about the child who will potentially join the household?
- How will the proposed new arrangements impact on the children already in the household?
- Are there any concerns about how their needs will continue to be met if a new child joins the family?

Interviews with children of the household

- What are the good things about living in your family?
- How were you asked about the child coming to live with you?
- What was your reaction to the idea?
- What do you think about that now?
- If the child is already living with you, how is that working out?
- What are the good things, and are there any bad things?
- What would you do if you were unhappy about the child living in your family?

UNDERTAKING A CONNECTED PERSON/FAMILY AND FRIENDS ASSESSMENT

- Are there people you could talk to outside the family?

If the applicant has children from a previous relationship who live elsewhere or grandchildren who visit and stay overnight, the questions can be adapted accordingly, and consideration given to interviewing those children.

When working with younger children, it may be helpful to use other communication methods to ascertain their views, such as drawing, worksheets, picture books or digital resources. Other specific communication techniques might be appropriate when working with disabled children.

ASSESSOR'S ANALYSIS

- **How well has the applicant involved their children in planning for the new child to potentially join the family?**
- **How is, or how would, a new child joining the family impact on children currently living in the household?**
- **Does the applicant have insight into how this change is impacting on them, or might impact on them?**
- **What are the views of children already in the household and have they been listened to?**
- **Are there any areas of vulnerability of children in the household, and if so what action could be taken to minimise this?**
- **Do children of the household have an outlet for expressing any concerns or worries?**
- **Do any of the children of the household need additional support to be provided?**

> **Verify through:**
> - **Interviews with the children (if of an age and understanding)**
> - **Personal references including from family members**
> - **School and nursery checks**
> - **Local authority checks**
> - **Social media checks**

Other adults in the household

- Give details of the other adult members of your household.
- Describe their relationship to and with you.
- Describe their relationship to and with the child whom you wish to care for.

- How would you describe them in terms of identity, personality, employment and experience of children?
- Have there been any incidents of domestic abuse involving household members?
- What is their attitude to the child potentially joining your household?
- What role would they be likely to play in caring for the child or providing support to you?
- Are there any issues that you would need to consider in relation to adult household members and keeping the child safe?

Interviews with adult household members

- What is your relationship to and with the child who may be joining the household?
- How much time do you spend with them or do you anticipate spending with them?
- How do you see your role in the family, especially in relation to child care?
- Do you have any concerns about the child joining the family?

ASSESSOR'S ANALYSIS

- **Is there evidence that these people could play a positive role in the child's life?**
- **Is there evidence that any of these people might pose a risk to the child, and if so, can the applicant keep the child safe?**
- **Does the applicant need any support in relation to managing these issues?**

> **Verify through:**
> - **Interviews with the children (if of an age and understanding)**
> - **Personal references including from family members**
> - **Disclosure and Barring Service (DBS) checks**
> - **Local authority checks**
> - **Social media checks**

Wider family/significant others

This section should include information about all other relevant family members who are not living in the household, including non-family members who might be significant in the life of the child (but it is not helpful to repeat information that may have already been provided in Section B of the Form C assessment report). For each person, the assessor should consider providing a brief pen picture describing personality, ethnicity and their current education or employment. It is important to provide information about the relationship between wider family and the applicant/s, and also with the child under consideration. Where relationships are tense, difficult or non-existent, this will need careful analysis. Children living outside of the home should normally be interviewed as part of the assessment.

The assessing social worker should have completed a family tree (see Appendix) as part of the front sheet paperwork. This will help the reader to understand the family composition and relationships.

- Give details of those who will have regular contact with the child, such as adult children, grandparents and others not living in the household.
- Describe their relationship to and with you.
- Describe their relationship to and with the child whom you wish to care for.
- How much contact would they be likely to have with the child?
- How would you describe them in terms of identity, personality, employment and experience of children?
- What is their attitude to the child potentially joining your household?
- Are there any issues that you would need to consider in relation to these people and keeping the child safe?

ASSESSOR'S ANALYSIS

- **Have wider family members and other significant people been interviewed?**
- **Is there evidence that these people could play a positive role in the child's life?**
- **Can the applicant sustain appropriate relationships with these adults in the best interests of the child?**
- **Is there evidence that any of these people might pose a risk to the child, and if so, can the applicant keep the child safe?**
- **Does the applicant need any support in relation to these issues?**

Relationships and network

> **Verify through:**
> - **Interviews with the children (if of an age and understanding)**
> - **Personal references including from family members**
> - **Social media checks**

Support network

The stresses of caring for children are well recognised, and carers often feel the benefits of support from family and friends. The issue of a support network will be particularly important for single applicants.

In this section, the assessor is required to set out the supportive relationships that exist within the applicant's network, and provide information about the type and quality of support that might be available. This needs to be specific and cover practical situations that are likely to emerge.

An ecomap (see Appendix) might be a useful tool, and is used to represent in a picture format the applicant/s and the connections that they have with others in their community. Assessors need to be clear that although an ecomap might be included as evidence, it is primarily a tool to aid discussion and reflection, and is not an end in itself.

- List the people who might be able to support you in caring for the child.
- Describe them in terms of their identity, their family composition, where they live, how often you see them, and the nature of the support that each might offer.
- Describe their relationship to and with you.
- Describe their relationship to and with the child whom you wish to care for.
- How often are they likely to visit the home and will they spend time alone with the child or young person?
- Provide details of any groups or organisations that you belong to and that might provide you with support.
- Where are you most likely to go for emotional support?
- Where are you most likely to go for practical support?
- Other than any partner, who do you feel closest to and why?
- Can you recall a recent stressful incident or issue? Who did you confide in and why? How helpful was it to do that?
- What would happen if you were unable to care for the child for any reason, in the short term or long term?

- Have you thought about how much information about the child you might share with those who might support you?
- What support would you be expecting from the local authority or other professionals, now and in the future?
- Are you aware of organisations such as Family Rights Group and Grandparents Plus that can offer independent external advice and support?

ASSESSOR'S ANALYSIS

- Do the applicant/s have adequate emotional support?
- Do the applicant/s have adequate practical support?
- If there are gaps in support, how might these be addressed?
- Is it possible and helpful to identify a "back-up" carer for unforeseen circumstances?
- What would happen if they were unable to care for the child for any reason, in the short term or long term?
- Is it necessary to interview any members of the support network?
- Do the applicant/s understand the circumstances in which it might be helpful to share information, and when it might be better to keep information confidential?
- Are the applicant/s willing to make use of local authority or other professional support that might be available?
- Are the applicant/s aware of organisations that can offer independent advice and support?

> **Verify through:**
> - Personal references including from family members
> - Interviews with members of the support network

Parenting capacity

5

Experience of caring for children

In this section, the assessor is asked to provide information about the applicant's experience of, and capacity for, caring for children generally. This may relate to birth children, children of friends or relatives, or children known in professional or other work capacities, but should not relate to the child or children that the applicant/s is being assessed to care for. This is covered in the subsequent section.

Evidence in relation to foster carers (Sinclair *et al*, 2005) identifies positive outcomes for those who were caring, accepting, encouraging, and able to see things from the child's perspective. These carers were good at listening to and talking to children and young people, and made time to undertake activities with the child, including teaching life skills. Where foster carers were apathetic, rejecting or intolerant, this was associated with poor outcomes. It is likely that this is also true of parenting more generally, and so will be a good indicator of strengths in family and friends carers. The same research also suggests that successful outcomes are most likely where foster carers are able to effectively offer routine and structure, have clear expectations, set boundaries and manage behaviour.

- Describe your experience of caring for your own or other children.
- What have been the rewards and challenges of doing this?
- Describe the quality of the relationship you have with children whom you have parented or cared for.
- Thinking of your own experience of being parented, what have you done differently as a parent, and what have you kept the same?
- How have you demonstrated warmth and affection towards children whom you have cared for?
- How have you helped children to achieve a good standard of physical and emotional health?
- What interests did the children have and how did you encourage these?
- How have you helped these children to attend school and to achieve their potential?

- How have you managed the behaviour of children whom you have cared for? How have you encouraged positive behaviour and rewarded children?

ASSESSOR'S ANALYSIS

- Is there evidence that the applicant has been successful in their parenting or caring for other children? How might this transfer to the child in question?
- Based on their previous child care experience, what would you identify as the applicant's strengths as a parent or carer?
- Based on their previous child care experience, do you have any concerns about the applicant's suitability as a parent or carer?

> **Verify through:**
> - **Interviews with birth children or other children whom the applicant has cared for**
> - **Personal references including from family members**
> - **Former partner references**
> - **School and nursery checks**

Applicant's relationship with the child

It is important to understand that in a family and friends assessment, the applicant/s are not being considered to foster a range of different children, but rather to care for a particular child or children, who is usually related to them. In many cases, they will know that child well, and it is the existing relationship with the child that is the main strength of the application. This means that while the assessment can and must take account of parenting capacity more generally, what really matters is their ability to care for the child under consideration, in the present and future, until the child reaches the age of 18 and beyond.

- How would you describe your relationship with the child or children whom you wish to care for?
- How do you think the child whom you wish to care for feels about living with you/coming to live with you?
- How do you demonstrate warmth and affection in your relationship with the child whom you wish to care for?
- How do you think your relationship with the child might develop as they get older?

Parenting capacity

- How do you demonstrate your long-term commitment to caring for the child?

ASSESSOR'S ANALYSIS

- **How would you describe the applicant's relationship with the child whom they wish to care for?**

- **Does the applicant appear able to understand the child's feelings and be able to empathise with the child?**

- **What evidence is there of warmth and affection in the relationship between the applicant and the child whom they wish to care for?**

- **Is the applicant realistic about the challenges of caring for the child or children as they get older?**

> **Verify through:**
> - **Interviews with the child (if of an age and understanding)**
> - **Personal references including from family members**
> - **School and nursery checks**

Ability to meet the needs of the child

This is arguably the most crucial section of the form in that it asks about an ability to meet the needs of the particular child under consideration. These needs will have been set out in Section A and this should form the basis of discussions. The research evidence is clear in that there are no links between outcomes for children and factors like the age, health, accommodation, or personal family history of the carer. What matters is parenting capacity, and an associated willingness and ability to meet the child's identified needs.

In many cases, it is relatively straightforward to show that the child's needs are being met in the present by the applicant/s, but where this is the plan, it is also necessary to show that the applicant/s is likely to be able to meet their needs until the child reaches the age of 18 and beyond.

- What did you know about the child's circumstances in the period leading up to them no longer living with their birth parents? Were you able to do anything to help?

- What do you think are the risks to the child now, and what do you think is needed to keep them safe?

- If the child has suffered harm, what do you think is necessary to help them recover from the effects of that harm?

- What do you think are the child's current and future needs relating to their identity, and how do you think you will be able to meet these?
- What do you think are the child's current and future needs relating to their health, and how do you think you will be able to meet these?
- Do you feel comfortable discussing issues such as drugs, alcohol and sexual health with the child, when the time is right?
- What do you think are the child's current and future needs relating to their education, and how do you think you will contribute to meeting these?
- What do you think are the child's current and future needs relating to their emotional and behavioural development, and how do you think you will be able to meet these?
- What techniques do you currently use to manage the child's behaviour?
- What boundaries do you think are important with teenagers and what techniques would you use to enforce these?
- How do you, or how will you, manage the use of the internet and social media with the child in order to keep them safe?

ASSESSOR'S ANALYSIS

- **What did the applicant/s know about the child's life in the period leading up to them no longer living with their birth parents?**
- **Were they able to do anything to help, and if not, why not?**
- **Does the applicant/s understand the potential risks to the child and are they capable of keeping them safe, now and in the future?**
- **Does the applicant/s have a good understanding of the needs of the child whom they wish to care for?**
- **Is there evidence that the applicant/s is likely to be able to meet those needs now and in the future?**
- **How realistic is the applicant/s about the challenges that teenagers can present, and do they have appropriate strategies to manage these?**
- **Is there any support or training that might be needed to help the applicant/s to meet the child's needs, now or in the future?**

> **Verify through:**
> - **Interviews with the child (if of an age and understanding)**
> - **Personal references including from family members**
> - **School and nursery checks**
> - **Feedback from other professionals involved with the child**

Contact and family relationships

Although the research literature tends to conclude that, on balance, family and friends care tends to achieve more frequent and consistent contact than arrangements with stranger foster carers (Hunt *et al*, 2008), this is not without difficulty. Alongside the challenges that would accompany any sort of contact planning, for family and friends carers additional complexities arise because of the carer's existing relationships with birth parents, often as parents or siblings.

Assessment in this area will need to consider the applicant's attitude to the birth parents and other family members, and their ability to promote appropriate and beneficial contact while at the same time protecting the child from any identified risk. The assessor will need to consider how applicants might promote contact with both sides of the family – maternal and paternal.

It should not be assumed that contact can always be managed by family and friends carers, and this is an area in which local authority support is often required, not least in some cases to protect carers from physical assault (Wellard, 2011). The requirement for support around contact is set out in statutory guidance, and Adams (2012, Chapter 7) sets out the issues for consideration in planning contact in kinship care.

- Do you understand the local authority's plans for contact between the child and their parents or other birth family?
- Why do you think that this contact is important for the child, and how can you support it?
- How do you think the child might feel before and after contact with their parents or other birth family?
- How will your relationship with the child's birth parents and other birth family impact on your ability to support contact?
- Will the nature and frequency of your current contact with the child's parents need to change? If so, how do you feel about that?
- How will you promote the child's sense of identity in terms of their relationship with birth parents and other birth family in between contact meetings?
- Is contact arranged in a way that is both child-centred and leaves you feeling safe from any threats or aggression?
- Do you understand the limits on contact as set out by the local authority, and are you able and willing to adhere to these restrictions?
- Do you or will you need any support with contact arrangements?
- What action would you take if you thought that the child was at risk or felt unhappy during contact?

ASSESSOR'S ANALYSIS

- Does the applicant/s understand the importance of contact, and are they willing to support the local authority's contact plans?
- Do they understand how to support the child in relation to contact meetings, but also in relation to relationships with birth parents and other family members more generally?
- Does the applicant/s demonstrate an understanding of how attending contact meetings might affect the child whom they wish to care for?
- Are the proposed contact arrangements child-centred and safe for all parties?
- Does or will the applicant/s need support from the local authority in managing or participating in contact arrangements?

> **Verify through:**
> - **Interviews with the child (if of an age and understanding)**
> - **Personal references including from family members**
> - **References from birth parents or information about their views**

Adams (2017) provides detailed guidance about checks and references in fostering and adoption and much of that is equally applicable to special guardianship assessments. An assessor using Form C should be familiar with that publication. It is important to understand that checks and references are an integral part of an assessment and cannot be seen as completely separate from the conversations that take place directly with the applicant/s.

DBS check

It is generally recognised that applicants should be asked at the earliest opportunity about any criminal offences that they may have committed, allowing them to be honest and to acknowledge their history in advance of a DBS check being completed. If the applicant/s admits or is subsequently found to have committed an offence, this will need to be discussed with them. This is also the case where a member of the household has committed an offence that may impact on a child living in that household.

- Have you or anyone in your household ever committed an offence that resulted in a conviction or caution?
- What was the offence and when did it happen?
- What were the circumstances surrounding the offence?
- What do you feel you have learned from the experience?
- How is this relevant to your suitability as a foster carer or special guardian?
- Are such offences likely to be repeated?
- Are you confident that the child whom you wish to care for will be safe in this household?

In general, individuals cannot be approved as foster carers if they have committed a range of offences as specified in regulation 26 of the Fostering Services Regulations 2011 (as amended). However, it is important to understand that this does not apply to relatives wanting to foster a particular child (regulation 26(8)).

> **ASSESSOR'S ANALYSIS**

- Does the applicant's offending history pose a risk to the child whom they wish to care for?
- Does the offending history of another household member pose a risk to the child whom they wish to care for?
- Can this risk be managed or is the applicant/s unsuitable to be a foster carer or special guardian for the child?

> **Verify through:**
> - DBS check
> - Personal references including from family members
> - Interviews with household members

Local authority check/previous applications to foster or adopt

Fostering Services Regulations 2011 (as amended) and Special Guardianship Regulations 2005 (as amended) require that a check be undertaken with the applicant's home local authority. Good practice requires that in some circumstances a check should also be undertaken with previous local authorities (Adams, 2017). Local authority checks will also provide information about previous applications to foster, adopt or childmind.

- Have you or any member of your household been involved with local authority children's services for any reason?
- If so, when, where and for what reason? What was the outcome of your involvement?
- Have you or any member of your household previously applied to become a foster carer, adopter or childminder?
- If so, who, when, where and what was the outcome?
- If you were not approved or withdrew, what were the reasons for that?
- If you were approved, but subsequently resigned or had your approval terminated, what were the events that led to this situation?

> **ASSESSOR'S ANALYSIS**
>
> - Has the applicant/s or any member of their household had any involvement with local authority children's services?
> - If so, what is the relevance of that in relation to their suitability to be a foster carer or special guardian for the child in question?
> - What is the relevance of any experiences as a foster carer, adopter or childminder for this application?

> **Verify through:**
> - **Local authority checks**
> - **Interviews with household members**
> - **References in relation to fostering, adoption or childminding**

Health

For fostering and special guardianship assessments, a report is required from a health practitioner. Good practice requires that this report is provided by a fostering service medical adviser or an equivalent health professional with a good understanding of the demands of providing family-based care in this context. The medical adviser comments can be set out in this section, or alternatively as a letter or report that is attached to the form. The assessor should ensure that the medical adviser's comments are provided in full, and they should not be summarised (except by that medical adviser) or interpreted.

It is recognised that caring for children of family and friends is challenging and demanding, and that this can have an adverse impact on foster carers' health. For example, we know that family and friends carers are older and have generally poorer health than unrelated foster carers. It is also the case that, like others in the population, they may, through lifestyle choices, smoke (BAAF, 2007), be overweight (Mather and Lehner, 2010), or consume alcohol above recommended levels. It is important that information about an applicant's health and lifestyle is carefully considered, and that assessors avoid being unfairly judgemental but instead focus on parenting capacity now and in the future. Assessors should understand that there is no research evidence to link the health of kinship carers with the outcomes for the children for whom they care (Hunt et al, 2008).

However, in some cases health issues may impact on an individual's ability to provide good care, and local authorities should consider what support might helpfully be provided in these circumstances. This might include providing information and advice to assist carers in taking good care of their own health, using health services appropriately and promoting a healthy lifestyle for the child in their care.

Adams (2017) addresses the issue of health assessments in some depth.

- What efforts do you make to try to maintain good health?
- Do you suffer from any significant illnesses or health issues, including mental health or stress-related issues (or did you in the past)?
- If so, what support do you have in place to manage these conditions or illnesses?
- Could these health issues impact on your ability to meet the needs of the child whom you wish to care for, now or in the future?
- What is your experience of and attitude to smoking, alcohol use, and use of drugs and illegal substances?
- If a medical has indicated that you are overweight, how will this impact on your ability to care for the child, now or in the future?
- Do you consider yourself an emotionally stable person? What makes you think that?
- Do any family members have health conditions or a disability that might impact on you being able to meet the needs of the child whom you wish to care for?

ASSESSOR'S ANALYSIS

- **How would you summarise the applicant's physical and mental health?**
- **What is the relevance of past or present ill-health (physical or mental) in terms of the applicant's ability to meet the needs of the child whom they wish to care for?**
- **How have issues about smoking, alcohol, substance use, or obesity been addressed?**
- **What can you conclude about the applicant's ability to manage the stress that is likely to accompany the role that they wish to take on?**
- **Does the applicant/s need any support to provide a healthy lifestyle for the child whom they wish to care for?**

> **Verify through:**
>
> - **Medical reports including from consultants and other health professionals**
> - **Personal references including from family members**
> - **Former partner references**
> - **Employer and former employer checks**

Home and neighbourhood

Special guardianship and fostering regulations require a description of the applicant's accommodation. This will include information about the general condition of the home that for fostering must be 'adequately furnished and decorated [and] maintained to a good standard of cleanliness and hygiene throughout' (National Minimum Standard (NMS) 10.2), and able to 'comfortably accommodate all who live there' (NMS 10.1).

Fostering standards require that in most circumstances, 'each child over the age of three should have their own bedroom' (NMS 10.6), although there is scope for some bedroom sharing if this is in line with the child's wishes and is agreed by their social worker. Statutory guidance makes clear that requirements for accommodation should be interpreted more flexibly for family and friends foster carers and, even if not ideal, should be seen in the context of a holistic assessment, and balanced against other factors.

- Is your home suitable for looking after the child whom you wish to care for?
- If not, what are your plans for addressing this matter?
- Will the child have their own bedroom?
- If not, what are the proposed sleeping arrangements?
- Will sleeping arrangements need to change as the child gets older?
- If your home is rented, is the landlord aware of your plans to look after this child?
- Do you give permission for us to write to the landlord?

In most circumstances, descriptions of the neighbourhood and community will be brief, although more detailed information may be necessary if, for example, the area has a known gang presence, is known for racial intolerance, or is very rural. The assessor will need to use their judgement in this respect.

- Describe your neighbourhood and the area that you live in.
- What resources and amenities does it have that would be relevant to the child whom you wish to care for, such as schools and GP surgeries?

If the applicant has a dog or pet then an assessment should be completed, and the information included in this section (see Adams, 2015).

ASSESSOR'S ANALYSIS

- **Is the accommodation suitable to meet the needs of the child?**
- **If relevant, is the landlord agreeable to the applicant/s caring for the child while living in this home?**
- **Are there any known risks or dangers to the child in the local community, and if so, how can these risks or dangers be minimised?**
- **What is the relevance of any information arising from a dog or pet assessment?**

UNDERTAKING A CONNECTED PERSON/FAMILY AND FRIENDS ASSESSMENT

- **If the accommodation is not suitable, can any support be provided to help with an extension or with moving house?**

> **Verify through:**
> - **Home safety check**
> - **Observations of the local area**
> - **Dog or pet assessment**
> - **Personal references**
> - **Written check with the landlord**

Income and expenditure

This section requires brief information about income and expenditure/standard of living, to the extent that it is relevant to an application to become a special guardian or foster carer.

- How would you describe your financial situation?
- What is your general attitude towards money and how do you manage your finances?
- If you are a couple, do you have similar or different attitudes to these matters?
- Does your financial position mean that your accommodation is secure?
- Do you have any debts, and if so, how are you managing these?
- Will taking on the care of this child require you to make changes to your employment?
- If so, what are the financial implications of that?
- Are you aware of any benefits or allowances that you might be entitled to and how they might be affected by your looking after this child?
- Are you planning any major changes (such as giving up or reducing work) that will impact on your financial situation?

ASSESSOR'S ANALYSIS

- **Does the applicant/s appear to be financially secure?**
- **Have they planned for any financial adjustments that will come with caring for the child?**

- Are any debts manageable and unlikely to create subsequent difficulties that impact on the child?

- Does the applicant/s need advice about benefits or allowances that they might be entitled to claim?

> **Verify through:**
> - Financial assessment
> - Employer checks

Previous family court proceedings

Special guardianship regulations require details of any previous family court proceedings involving the applicant/s, and this information will likely also be relevant to fostering applications. It may be appropriate to take legal advice in order to try and get a copy of the relevant court paperwork for these proceedings.

- Have you ever been involved in previous family court proceedings?
- If so, when and where, and what were they about?
- What was the outcome of these proceedings?

ASSESSOR'S ANALYSIS

- If the applicant/s has been involved with previous family court proceedings, how are these relevant to their current suitability as a foster carer or special guardian?

Personal references

Fostering Services Regulations 2011 require that the assessor interviews at least two persons nominated by the prospective foster carers, and prepares a written report based on the information gathered (unless the applicant/s has been a foster carer within the previous 12 months and a reference has been provided). Good practice has led to most fostering services requiring at least one additional reference, and many fostering services require more than that. Special guardianship regulations require three personal references.

UNDERTAKING A CONNECTED PERSON/FAMILY AND FRIENDS ASSESSMENT

Personal references can provide hugely important information, coming as they do from people who usually know the applicant/s extremely well. Family members are a rich source of evidence and it is good practice to interview them all if this is possible, although this is not always appropriate where there are difficult family dynamics. Where possible, it is also helpful to take references from individuals who are outside of the family network.

- How long have you known the applicant/s and in what capacity?
- How frequently do you have contact with them now, and did you in the past?
- What have the applicant/s told you about the child whom they wish to care for and their circumstances?
- Please describe the personal qualities that you feel the applicant/s have that are relevant to caring for this child.
- Please comment on the quality and stability of the adult relationships within the applicant's household.
- If the applicant/s have children living at home, how would you describe them? How do you think they might respond to living with the child whom the applicant/s wish to care for?
- What have you observed of the applicant's relationships with the child whom they wish to care for and/or with their own children?
- What have you observed or what do you know about the applicant's relationship with other family members?
- What can you say about the ability of the applicant/s to manage stress?
- Have you ever been aware that the applicant/s have used smacking, physical chastisement or any inappropriate discipline to manage children's behaviour?
- Please comment on the applicant's ability to work effectively with others as part of a team.
- Please comment on the applicant's honesty, trustworthiness and ability to keep sensitive information confidential.
- What do you think will be their biggest challenges in caring for this child?
- Are there any areas where you think the applicant/s might need support?
- Do you know anything that makes you think the applicant/s might not be suitable to care for this child?
- Would you have any concerns about the safety or well-being of this child if they were placed in their care?
- Is there any other information that you want to share?

ASSESSOR'S ANALYSIS

- **Do the references support a view of the applicant/s as suitable to care for this child?**
- **How much weight do you give to the references and why?**

- **Do the references confirm what is evident from other aspects of the assessment or do they contradict this?**

- **Do the references give raise to any concerns that need further exploration?**

- **Do the references indicate any support that might be necessary for the applicant/s?**

Other checks and references

These might include former partner checks, employer or former employer checks, school or nursery checks, or social media checks. Adams (2017) considers these issues in some detail and assessors should be familiar with that text.

Former partner checks

Adams (2017) sets out the importance of undertaking checks with former partners, provides a form for recording these (Former Partner Reference, in Appendices), and discusses the practicalities and issues to consider in developing a policy on this. Former partner checks are now established as routine good practice in the context of fostering, especially where an applicant has jointly parented or cared for a child with a former partner. In these circumstances, former partners will usually be well placed to verify information provided by the applicant/s, or to provide further information about the applicant's parenting capacity. Where former partners have not jointly parented or cared for a child, but have been in a significant relationship, they may still be well placed to provide important information about the applicant/s.

It is less common to undertake such checks in relation to special guardianship, although arguably the benefits in a fostering context apply equally to this legal order. Each local authority should have a policy setting out the requirement for former partner checks, for both fostering and special guardianship, and applicants should be informed of this at an early stage in the assessment.

Employer checks

It is now routine practice in fostering to undertake employer checks, and good practice suggests that all current employers should be contacted to confirm the information given by the applicant/s about their employment, and to gather evidence regarding their suitability to care for a family member or friend. CoramBAAF has developed a form for recording this information (Employer/Voluntary Activity Reference in the Appendices of Adams, 2017). Where applicants are involved in voluntary work, this should be considered in the same way as paid employment. The same arguments about the importance of such checks can be equally applied to special guardianship assessments. Each local authority should have a policy about requirements in relation to undertaking employer checks for both fostering and special guardianship.

Former employer checks

Good practice in fostering recognises that any previous employers should be contacted if an applicant was working with children or vulnerable adults, to ensure that there were no safeguarding or protection concerns, and to gather evidence regarding their suitability. Where applicants were involved in voluntary work with children or vulnerable adults, this should be considered in the same way as paid employment, and can provide valuable evidence about child care skills. Each local authority should have a policy about requirements in relation to undertaking previous employer, volunteering or student checks for both fostering and special guardianship assessments.

School and nursery checks

Good practice in fostering requires checks to be undertaken if the children of applicant/s are attending school or nursery. CoramBAAF publishes a form for recording this information (School and Nursery Reference, in the Appendices of Adams, 2017). These checks should not focus on the achievements or otherwise of the particular children, but should attempt to gather information about how well the applicant/s supports the child in these settings, and how well they work with professionals in this context. Each local authority will require a policy setting out requirements in this area.

Social media checks

Fostering and adoption services are increasingly making checks using social networking websites and internet search engines, and each local authority should have a policy in this regard, covering assessments of special guardians (see Adams, 2017 for more information).

Other checks

Other checks in this section might include overseas police checks when applicants have spent long periods living abroad, checks with the NSPCC, checks with probation services, Protection of Children checks for applicants who have lived in Northern Ireland, or Disclosure checks for applicants who have lived in Scotland (see Adams, 2017 for more information).

Section D of Form C consists of three different forms, one for each of the three legal frameworks for which the form was designed. The assessor will only need to complete one of them, depending on whether the recommendation is in relation to the connected person being deemed suitable for temporary fostering approval, special guardianship, or as a foster carer.

In some circumstances, it is possible that connected persons might be considering other legal arrangements such as adoption or a child arrangements order. There may be good reasons for this, and each case should be considered according to the specific individual circumstances that apply.

Understanding the legal framework

It is important that the assessor takes into account the views and wishes of the prospective carer in terms of what they consider to be the most suitable legal framework. This will inevitably include discussions to check that they have a good understanding of the differences between the legal orders.

- What do you understand to be the main differences between the various legal orders available to you?

- Which of these legal orders do you think would best suit you and the child whom you wish to care for? Why do you think this?

- Have you been provided with information to read about the different legal options?

- Have you had independent advice about this from a legal representative or from an organisation like Family Rights Group or Grandparents Plus?

ASSESSOR'S ANALYSIS

- **Does the applicant/s understand the key differences between the different legal orders?**

- **Can they clearly explain their preference for being a special guardian, foster carer or adopter, and the reasons for that?**
- **Does the applicant/s need legal advice or advice from an independent organisation to help them consider their position?**

Special guardianship

For connected persons, special guardianship is commonly the most popular legal order, but it is important that they understand the advantages and disadvantages of this compared with foster care or adoption.

- Do you understand the implications of sharing parental responsibility for the child with birth parents?
- Are you aware of what practical support will be available to you under special guardianship, and how this compares with fostering?
- Are you aware of what financial support will be available to you under special guardianship, and how this compares with fostering?
- What is proposed in terms of contact with birth parents or other family members, and what support will you need with that?

ASSESSOR'S ANALYSIS

- Does the applicant/s have a realistic understanding of how being a special guardian is different from being a parent, adopter or a foster carer?
- Has the applicant/s considered what support they might need and the extent to which this will be available as a special guardian?
- In particular, have they considered financial issues and how they might be able to manage contact with birth parents or other family members?

> **Verify through:**
> - **Feedback from any information events or preparation training that have been attended by the applicant**

Fostering

Foster carers are expected to function within a set of regulations, standards and policies and procedures. They will be expected to work closely with their supervising social worker and the range of professionals involved with a child in care: social worker, reviewing officer, and professionals from health and education backgrounds. If approval as a foster carer is recommended as the most appropriate, it is important to be clear that the applicant/s understands the implications of this, and that they will comply with the requirements that go with it.

- Have you been offered any preparation training in relation to fostering, or been provided with any written information?

- What do you think will be the expectations of you as a foster carer?

- Do you understand what will be required in terms of supervision, reviews, training, and record-keeping?

- As a foster carer, which professionals involved with the care of the child will you need to work alongside?

- Can you think of times in your life when you have worked with child care professionals or as part of a team?

- What is your experience of any contact you may have had with the local authority to date, and what does that say about how easy it will be to work with them as a foster carer?

- How do you manage disagreements and do you understand that as a foster carer you will not have parental responsibility for the child in your care?

ASSESSOR'S ANALYSIS

- **Does the applicant/s have a realistic understanding of the role of a foster carer and what is expected of them?**

- **Is the applicant/s going to be able to meet those expectations?**

- **Will the applicant/s be able to work effectively with the range of child care professionals?**

- **Will it be possible to manage differences of opinion in the best interests of the child whom they wish to care for?**

- **Has the local authority offered appropriate preparation training or provided the applicant/s with written material about fostering?**

- **Are the requirements of the local authority realistic and appropriate for family and friends foster carers, or do they need to be reviewed?**

Verify through:

- **Feedback from any information events or preparation training that have been attended by the applicant**

Adams P (2012) *Planning for Contact in Permanent Placements*, London: BAAF

Adams P (2015) *Dogs and Pets in Fostering and Adoption*, London: BAAF

Adams P (2017) *Undertaking Checks and References in Fostering and Adoption Assessments*, London: CoramBAAF

BAAF (2007) *Reducing the Risks of Environmental Tobacco Smoke for Looked After Children and their Carers*, Practice Note 51, London: BAAF

Beesley P (2015) *Making Good Assessments*, London: CoramBAAF

Betts B (2007) *A Marginalised Resource? Recruiting, assessing and supporting single carers*, London: BAAF

Department for Education (2011) *Family and Friends Care: Statutory guidance for local authorities*, London: DfE

Family Rights Group (2010) *Family and Friends Care: A guide to good practice for local authorities in England*, London: Family Rights Group

Family Rights Group and Expert Working Group (2017) *Initial Family and Friends Care Assessment: A good practice guide*, London: Family Rights Group, available at: www.frg.org.uk/involving-families/family-and-friends-carers/assessment-tool

Farmer E and Moyers S (2008) *Kinship Care: Fostering effective family and friends placements*, London: Jessica Kingsley Publishers

Harrington K (2017) *Serious Case Review: Child A and Child B*, Oxfordshire Safeguarding Children Board, available at: www.oscb.org.uk/wp-content/uploads/Child-A-and-Child-B-OSCB-Overview-Report-March-2017-1.pdf

Hunt J, Waterhouse S and Lutman E (2008) *Keeping them in the Family: Outcomes for children placed in kinship care through care proceedings*, London: BAAF

Hunt J and Waterhouse S (2012) 'Parental contact for children placed in kinship care through care proceedings', *Child and Family Law Quarterly*, 22:1, pp 71–92

Mather M and Lehner K (2010) *Evaluating Obesity in Substitute Carers*, London: BAAF

Roth D, Aziz R, Lindley B and Ashley C (eds) (2012) *Understanding Family and Friends Care: Local authority policies – the good, the bad and the non-existent*, London: Family Rights Group

Bibliography

Roth D, Lindley B and Ashley C (2011) *Big Bruv, Little Sis*, London: Family Rights Group

Roth D, Tunnard J, Lindley B, De Gaye A and Ashley C (2011) *Managing Contact*, London: Family Rights Group

Selwyn J, Farmer E, Meakings S and Vaisey P (2013) *The Poor Relations? Children and informal kinship carers speak out*, Bristol: University of Bristol

Simmonds J (2011) *The Role of Special Guardianship: Best practice in permanency planning for children (England and Wales)*, London: BAAF

Sinclair I, Wilson K and Gibbs I (2005) *Foster Placements: Why they succeed and why they fail*, London: Jessica Kingsley Publishers

Staunton A (2016) *Serious Case Review: Bonnie*, Devon: Devon Safeguarding Children Board

Talbot C and Calder M (eds) (2006) *Assessment in Kinship Care*, Lyme Regis: Russell House Publishing

Tarrant A, Featherstone B, O'Dell L and Fraser C (2017) '"You try to keep a brave face on but inside you are in bits": grandparent experiences of engaging with professionals in children's services', *Qualitative Social Work*, 16:3, pp 351–366

Wade J, Dixon J and Richards A (2010) *Special Guardianship in Practice*, London: BAAF

Wade J, Sinclair I, Stuttard L and Simmonds J (2014), *Investigating Special Guardianship: Experiences, outcomes and challenges*, London: DfE

Wate R (2017) *Serious Case Review: Shi-Anne Downer (Birth Name) AKA Keegan Downer*, Birmingham: Birmingham Safeguarding Children Board, available at: www.lscbbirmingham.org.uk/images/SCR_BSCB_2015-16-02.pdf

Wellard S (2011) *Too Old to Care? The experiences of older grandparents raising their grandchildren*, London: Grandparents Plus

Wellard S and Wheatley B (2010) *Family and Friends Care: 'What if we said no?'* London: Grandparents Plus

Wiffin J (2017) *Serious Case Review: Child J 13.04.2017*, Nottingham: Nottingham City Safeguarding Children Board, available at: http://gossweb.nottinghamcity.gov.uk/documents/Child%20J%20SCR%20Report%20April%202017.pdf

Drawing a family tree

Family tree symbols

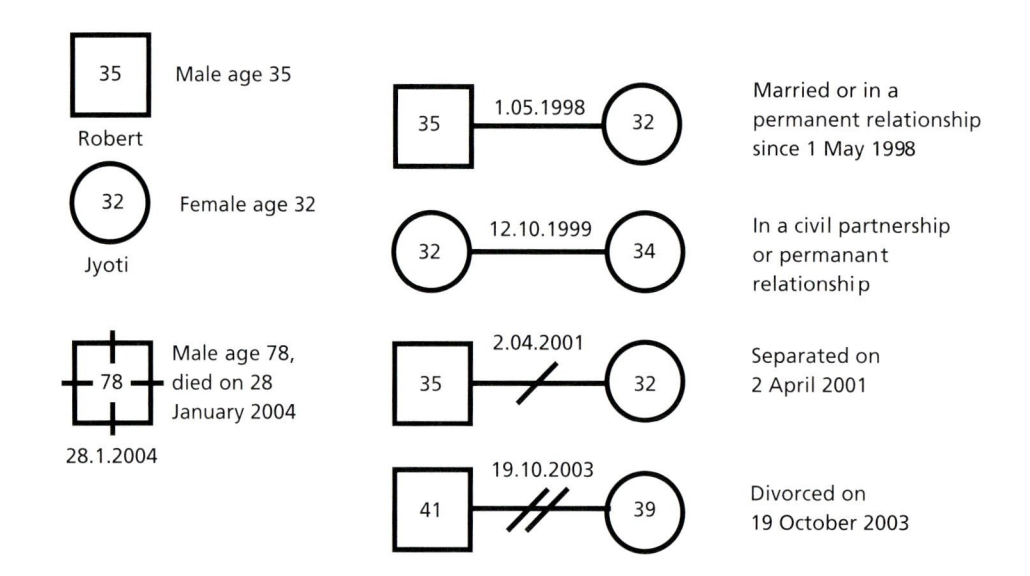

[35] Robert	Male age 35	[35]—1.05.1998—(32)	Married or in a permanent relationship since 1 May 1998
(32) Jyoti	Female age 32	(32)—12.10.1999—(34)	In a civil partnership or permanant relationship
[78] 28.1.2004	Male age 78, died on 28 January 2004	[35]—2.04.2001 /—(32)	Separated on 2 April 2001
		[41]—19.10.2003 //—(39)	Divorced on 19 October 2003

Appendix: family tree and ecomap

Example of a family tree

Robert and Jyoti's family tree

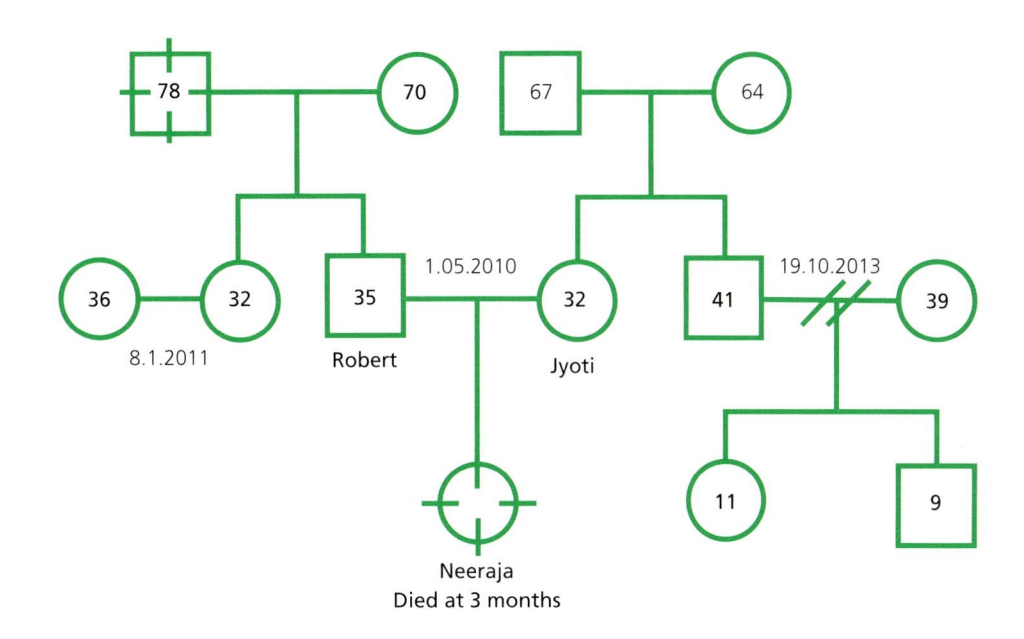

Drawing an ecomap

An ecomap is used to represent in a picture format an individual or couple, and their connections or relationships with family, friends, and others in the community. These connections can be drawn in such a way as to indicate the quality and energy that make up these connections. Used in conjunction with a family tree, ecomaps contain a large amount of information about an individual's relationships and social networks on just two pages.

Ecomaps are drawn by placing the family household at the centre of the drawing and then enclosing this in a circle. The symbols identified previously on drawing family trees should be used to do this.

Individuals then identify the people with whom they have relationships outside of the household and this should include groups or organisations in the community that are of significance. These should be defined in a broad way so that individuals or groups not in the immediate geographical vicinity can be shown if they are significant.

Connections should then be made between individuals in the household and individuals, groups and organisations using the following lines.

———————	A strong connection
— — — — — —	A tenuous connection
‖‖‖‖‖‖‖‖‖‖‖‖‖‖‖‖‖	A stressful connection

Appendix: family tree and ecomap

Example of an ecomap

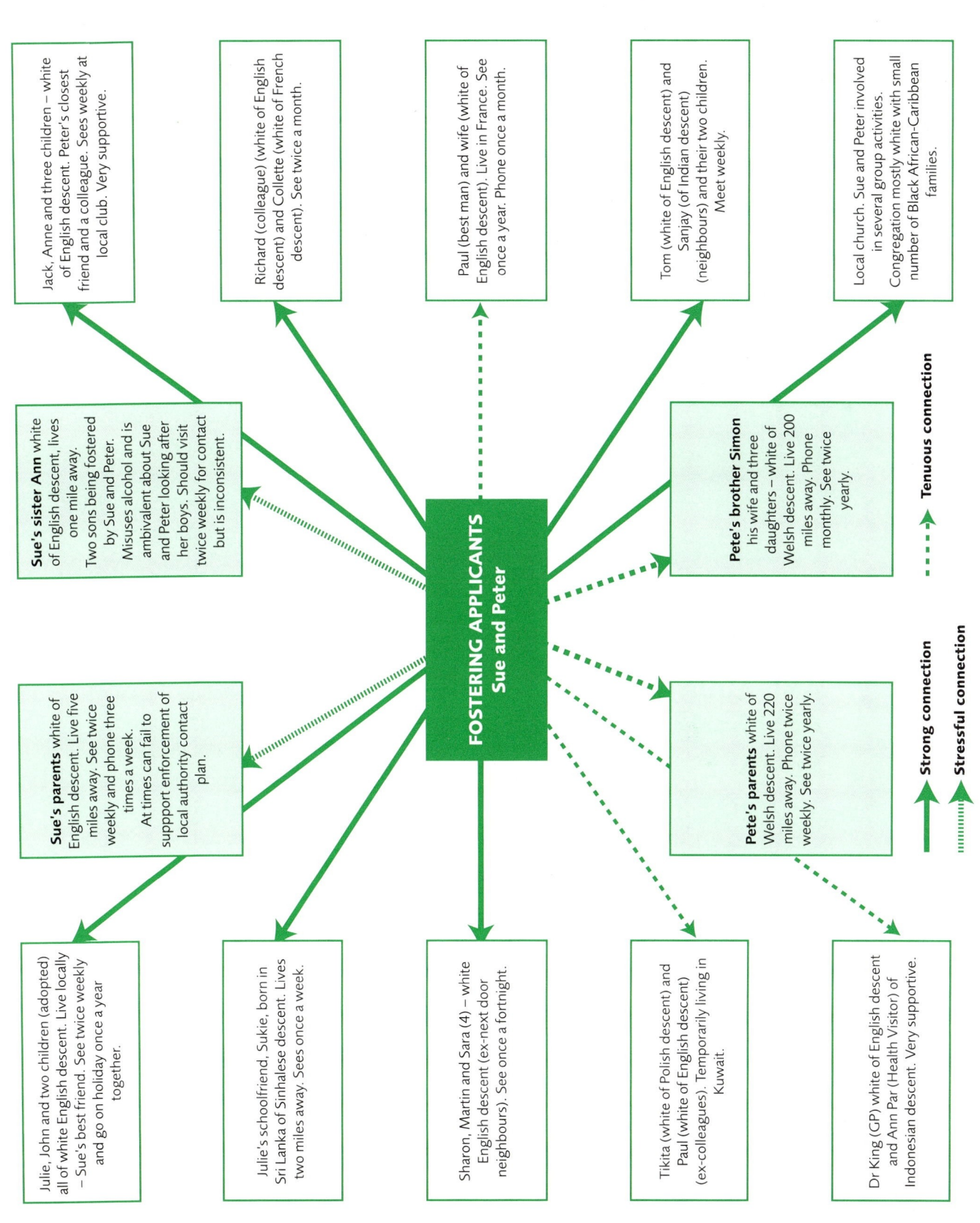

FOSTERING APPLICANTS: Sue and Peter

Sue's sister Ann white of English descent, lives one mile away. Two sons being fostered by Sue and Peter. Misuses alcohol and is ambivalent about Sue and Peter looking after her boys. Should visit twice weekly for contact but is inconsistent.

Sue's parents white of English descent. Live five miles away. See twice weekly and phone three times a week. At times can fail to support enforcement of local authority contact plan.

Pete's brother Simon his wife and three daughters – white of Welsh descent. Live 200 miles away. Phone monthly. See twice yearly.

Pete's parents white of Welsh descent. Live 220 miles away. Phone twice weekly. See twice yearly.

Jack, Anne and three children – white of English descent. Peter's closest friend and a colleague. Sees weekly at local club. Very supportive.

Richard (colleague) (white of English descent) and Collette (white of French descent). See twice a month.

Paul (best man) and wife (white of English descent). Live in France. See once a year. Phone once a month.

Tom (white of English descent) and Sanjay (of Indian descent) (neighbours) and their two children. Meet weekly.

Local church. Sue and Peter involved in several group activities. Congregation mostly white with small number of Black African-Caribbean families.

Julie, John and two children (adopted) all of white English descent. Live locally – Sue's best friend. See twice weekly and go on holiday once a year together.

Julie's schoolfriend, Sukie, born in Sri Lanka of Sinhalese descent. Lives two miles away. Sees once a week.

Sharon, Martin and Sara (4) – white English descent (ex-next door neighbours). See once a fortnight.

Tikita (white of Polish descent) and Paul (white of English descent) (ex-colleagues). Temporarily living in Kuwait.

Dr King (GP) white of English descent and Ann Par (Health Visitor) of Indonesian descent. Very supportive.

Strong connection ──▶
Tenuous connection ┄┄▶
Stressful connection ┅┅▶

49

Undertaking Checks and References in Fostering and Adoption Assessments
The essential guide for practitioners

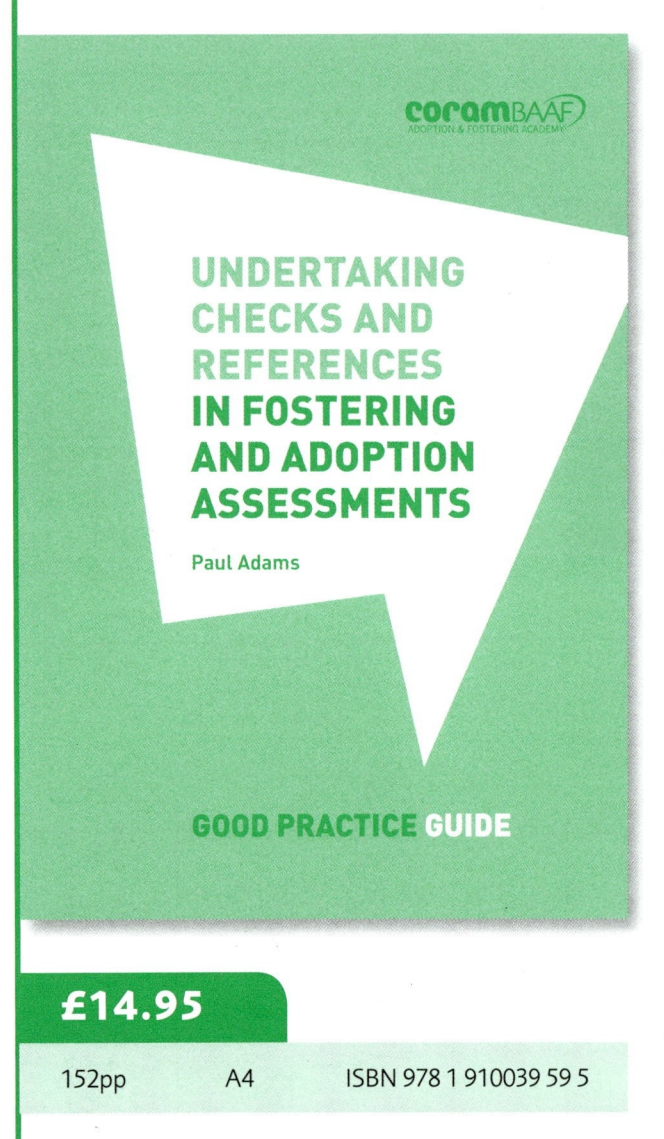

The assessment of prospective foster carers and adopters is amongst the most important aspects of family placement work. Undertaking checks and references is a key part of these assessments, and a core task for social workers. But which checks are mandatory, and which are advisable? Which checks are needed in each UK country? Which are likely to yield the most useful information?

This Good Practice Guide details the range of checks routinely undertaken in England, Scotland, Northern Ireland and Wales, in both fostering and adoption. It considers: what information can be gleaned from each check; in what circumstances various checks should be undertaken and when might they be deemed unnecessary; what services and agencies should consider when formulating policies in this area; and the practical steps to effectively undertake these checks.

This book will be invaluable for all those involved in undertaking checks and references, in either fostering or adoption, throughout the UK, and for those formulating policy and practice in this area.

£14.95

152pp   A4   ISBN 978 1 910039 59 5

Available from www.corambaaf.org.uk/bookshop